MARIA FRANKLAND

# Write your Life Story in a Year

*Turn your writing dream into reality*

AUTONOMY

PRESS

*This book was professionally typeset on Reedsy.*
*Find out more at reedsy.com*

*Write your Life Story in a Year*

*A story that's unique and true: no one can write it, except for you*

# Contents

# Join my 'Keep in Touch' list!

If you'd like to be kept in the loop about new books and special offers, join my 'keep in touch' list, and receive a free booklet, 'The 7 S.E.C.R.E.T.S. to Achieving your Writing Dreams,' visit www.mariafrankland.co.uk

This book is derived from a year-long online course which includes video, access to an online support group, further writing tasks and examples, links to further reading and the option of one-to-one support.

See https://mariafrankland.co.uk/write-your-life-story/ for more information.

# Introduction

I believe that everyone has an exciting and unique story to tell and you might be someone who has heard the words 'you should write a book.'

There are many people who aspire to write their life story and there is no doubt about what a huge accomplishment it is. However, many would-be autobiographers cite, 'I wouldn't know how to approach it,' or 'I never finish anything I start' as reasons why they never begin. This is where I come in!

This book has been derived from a successful class-taught and online course, which has been tried and tested by many new writers. It has ensured they go from the planning process, choosing what to include, through to the hugely enjoyable creation of recreating memory after memory. Scenes are built into chapters and before long, completion of that all-important first draft comes into being.

As well as supporting the creation of your autobiography or memoir this book will develop your writing craft and your talent as a writer. It will give you the tools you will need to polish your first draft until it is good enough to be published. I write this as a creative writing teacher with an MA in Creative Writing, and of course, as a multi-published author myself.

If you were taking this course in one of my face-to-face groups, o online, we would do one section every fortnight, but because this is a book, you can go as fast or as slow as you like, though I would impress on you, to take your time, and revisit the exercises several times. To thoroughly understand the material presented, spend at least the prescribed two weeks on each chapter and come back periodically to a chapter, to refresh yourself.

There are publications that promise a completed book in less time than a year, but speaking from experience, I know that a year is a realistic ambition.

The book has been divided into thirty sections with a view, as mentioned, to a fortnight being spent on each section. But you will probably find that you complete the earlier 'planning' sections much more quickly than the later ones, to have your book completed within the twelve months.

Underpinning this book is the requirement to write at least two scenes, memories or anecdotes every week. Doing this for fifty-two weeks will ensure completion of one hundred and four completed scenes. This, if divided into chapters containing four scenes, will result in an impressive twenty chapter book over the year.

You can complete your life story using this book solely as your guide, but there is also a companion workbook available to support the tasks and activities and give you space to reflect and to plan. Wherever you see [cwb] (companion workbook,) in the text, you will know there is a section in the accompanying workbook, available separately, for you to write in.

At the time of writing, I am working on my second memoir and I promise you there is rarely a better feeling than holding your published book in your hands.

Completion of your life story might be the dream, but the journey is just as enjoyable and rewarding as the destination. So enjoy every minute of it and I look forward to helping you all the way from planning to publication.

# Reflecting on Your Life

Welcome to Life Story in a Year! I'm so excited that you've chosen this book to support you on your journey. I bet you can't wait to get started. If you'd like to be supported by the companion workbook [cwb], it is available on Amazon.

First things first, consider whether you are going to write a **memoir** which focuses on an aspect or slice of your life, or an **autobiography** which is your story from birth up until the present day.

Let us now consider why people decide to tell their own stories.

**Why do people write autobiographically?**

- Therapy?
- Escapism and creativity?
- Enjoyment of recapturing a moment?
- To pass on a story/wisdom/lessons learned?
- To set the record straight?
- For financial gain?
- To offer a snapshot of an era or perspective?
- To leave something of themselves behind?

[cwb1.1] **But most importantly – why do <u>you</u> want to write auto-biographically?**

There might be several reasons, but the one that you first think of will probably be the main driver that keeps you going through this year-long process.

[cwb1.2] **What is your favourite autobiography?**

If autobiographies are not normally something you would read, consider reading in their entirety, at least two very different ones, in the duration of this course. Perhaps one written by a celebrity, and one written by a non-celebrity with a unique angle on an experience. The structure and techniques will infiltrate your own work.

I always advise writers taking my courses, whether in the classroom, through distance learning or by following one of my books, that the greatest investment they can make in their writing careers is reading the work of other writers. It really does make a huge difference.

**What makes an autobiography interesting?**

Maybe what most interests you as a reader will be the angle you use to tell your story. Of course, there can be more than one, and the suggestions I give you throughout the book are not exhaustive – you can add to them.

- Triumph over adversity. *Who doesn't love this sort of story?*
- An inspirational story. *Something which causes a reader to take action in their own life.*
- A journey. *The strongest stories offer an element of change between th*

*start and the end.*

- Relatability. *If we can relate to a story, it can be cathartic and even more interesting.*
- The addressing of an issue. *Particularly when it has been overcome – it can enable a reader to feel less alone in something they are experiencing.*
- The providing of insight into a unique situation. *Let's face it – we humans are nosy.*
- The showing of an era or a place. *A story offering atmosphere and description can enable us to experience something or somewhere we wouldn't otherwise.*

## What will make your autobiography interesting?

As you embark on the planning process, what makes your story unique?

I am now going to offer some questions to get you thinking more about this.

[cwb1.3] **Your responses to the following questions will offer some starting points for you:**

What unique experiences and events have you lived through? *Perhaps someone has said, "you should write a book?" Why have they said that?*

What places have you visited or lived in that others may be interested in?

What people in your life have had the most impact on you?

What is a motto you live by that you would like to pass forward to others? *This should be your 'ethos,' e.g. 'Don't Give Up,' and will form the central tone of your story.*

What sort of books do you enjoy reading? *What you like to read might become the tone of what you write,* For example, if you enjoy reading comedy, you might take a humorous approach in your own writing.

Romance, Family Drama, Adventure, Classic,
   Mystery, Thriller, Science Fiction, Crime,
   Historical, Fantasy, Young Adult, Comedy.

Who would you want to read your book? *Are you writing just for yourself, your family, or anyone in the world who wants to read it?*

Right, let's get you writing! That is, after all what you are here for! The writing prompts below focus on childhood, so if you are planning to include your childhood in your book, you can include them as scenes.

[cwb1.4] **Choose two or more of these writing prompts:**

- Who was your best childhood friend? Write about what you did together.
- Describe a favourite childhood toy – what feelings does it bring up now?
- What childhood event made you feel anxious or scared?
- Describe some wisdom/advice given to you as a child. Have you passed it on?
- Did you have any family traditions?

**Below are some suggestions as you proceed with the course:**

- Buy yourself a 'special' A4 notebook and pen which you will keep only for your writing – make it a hardback one with a design you love.

- Begin carrying a notebook and pen around with you - you never know when you might remember something or have an important conversation with a family member or someone who can contribute an interesting memory you will be able to use.

# Re-acquainting Yourself as the Main Character in Your Story

This is probably my favourite part of the planning process. It's one that many writers, especially those writing from real-life experience, might be tempted to skip. However, people change considerably over time. That applies to you, as the main character, as well as the secondary characters you will include in your story. This re-acquainting process is therefore important, as all your characters should be multi-dimensional in order for readers to care about them.

**The following elements help to create a reader connection with a character:**

Lots of different aspects to their personality, being relatable, information about their background, relationships – past and present, their mannerisms, their appearance, positive and negative behaviours, their rationales, morals and views on life, their goals, personality flaws, sense of humour and what their voice sounds like.

You will hopefully find it lots of fun to become as acquainted with yourself as you were then, before you bring yourself, as the main character, to the page. And the younger you are, when being brought to the page, the more fun the process will be. You should be able to recal yourself then, and hear yourself speak, whilst remembering what made you 'tick.' This will make it easier for readers to form an emotional connection to you and your story. And it is this emotional connection to yourself and all your other characters which will keep your readers turning the pages.

The prompts given below will help you re-familiarise yourself with your younger self, even if lots of these details do not make it into your book. The exercise will help you re-connect with the child or person you once were. This might sound a bit 'out there,' but trust me, it works!

## [cwb2.1] Putting Yourself onto the Page (At your Story's Starting Point)

- Name/Age, Home and Family Information:
- Medical Conditions:
- Something you have inherited:
- Favourite Food/Drink:
- Sleeping Patterns:
- Favourite Clothes:
- Something you do that 'bothers' others:
- Hobbies and Interests:
- Two things you did yesterday:
- One thing you plan to do tomorrow:
- A talent you have been told you possess:
- Something you are embarrassed about:
- Something you have always wanted to do:
- The most special thing you own:
- Something or someone that makes you laugh:
- The hardest thing you have ever had to do:
- Something you are scared of:

- Your happiest memory:
- Your favourite place:
- Something you once did that was helpful:

[cwb2.2] **Internal Monologue:** Introduce yourself, as though you are speaking at the time of the start of your story.

When you read this monologue aloud, the way you speak will help you become even more re-acquainted with who you used to be. (monologue means one person speaking.)

# Secondary Characters

It is important to also 'flesh out' your secondary characters and show their motivations and agendas.

This helps to ensure your book is well-rounded and realistic. A large part of what will create reader interest are the interactions between your characters.

[cwb3.1] **Bring at least two, or more, of your most prominent secondary characters back to life** at the age they were at the start of your story, using the prompts below.

- Name/age (at start of story):
- Appearance:
- Relationship and involvement in your story:
- What are your feelings towards each other?
- What is their goal and motivation?
- What is standing in their way?
- Back story:
- Again, read the monologue at the end out loud so you can hear their voices.
- The way you speak will help you become even better reacquainted with who they used to be.

[cwb3.2] **Complete a 'spider-gram'** with you at the centre and the secondary characters around you, with lines drawn to show relationships between you and them and them to each other. Focus on the key characters who have played a major role in your life story.

Enjoy this process of reconnecting with your characters as they were. Make sure you bring yourself and them to the page, as fully rounded, multi-dimensional characters with flaws, positive traits, goals and agendas.

Don't forget to keep a notebook on you at all times. Give yourself plenty of space for ideas and memories to rumble around. A notebook will ensure that you catch them before they are forgotten again.

# Atmospheric Settings

Now that your characters are ready to be 'introduced' to the page, it's time to place them in a location.

**The importance of setting in story:**

*You may want to add to this list.*

Human relationships don't occur in a vacuum – they have to take place in an environment. A character will move around their setting as they act and interact.

Settings can tell us about the era of the story. This is show and tell at its best. For example, if we talk about a twin tub washing machine, the reader will know something of the time it is being set in.

Settings can tell us about other issues prevalent in the story, such as poverty.

Good setting descriptions can pull the reader into the story and really how them what is going on. A reader can really be there.

A character's relationship with the setting, particularly their feelings about it can add to the story. This is powerful when a character doesn't want to be somewhere.

### How writers can use setting.

A cinematic approach can provide a more visual experience. Imagine the scene being 'staged.'

'Drip feed' the setting details through the narrative, rather than given in one dense paragraph. More on this later.

All the senses should be used – smell is particularly evocative.

We should also aim for atmosphere – for example darkness, temperature and physical reaction to a place.

**A useful starting point is to look at how published writers have used setting.**

Choose three books, preferably autobiography or memoir, and focus on one of the settings the author has brought to life.

[cwb4.1] For each one you choose, consider the following and make notes:

1.  What relationship exists between character and place?
2.  What has the writer focused on? Why do you think this is?
3.  How are sensory and physical impressions evoked?
4.  How is mood and emotion created?

Now the exciting bit – it's time to turn your attention to the setting you will use at the start of your book. Perhaps you have a photograph. If not, the internet might help.

[cwb4.2] **First, jot down a description of your initial setting, bringing in the senses.**

By now, you ought to have started to think about the period of time your story will span. If not, consider this briefly before continuing.

[cwb4.3] **Then, make a list of the main settings you will include in your story** – as many as you can think of.

[cwb4.4] **Now, put your character (you!)** into your setting and write a scene that may or may not find its way into your book – you should write this scene in the era/time of your life story's starting point- so now is the time to throw in that twin tub!

1. Enter the setting, (at the age you were.) Use a verb to portray your mood.
2. Look at something which triggers a memory. (Recent or distant.)
3. 'Do' something. Have your character, (you,) performing an action.
4. Have one of your secondary characters enter the setting and a dialogue take place between yourselves. (We will cover dialogue in the next section.) This is another opportunity to get to know one of your secondary characters better.
5. Leave the setting, thinking something as you go.

Don't *think* too much beforehand about what you are going to write – rather write what initially comes to mind. At this stage, everything is first draft. It's a time for you to be creative and unleash your story onto the page or screen.

You don't have to worry about anything but growing your word count and experimenting with all the different elements of writing as we go along. There will be plenty of time for tidying everything up later.

# How to Use Dialogue to Bring Your Writing to Life

Dialogue is one of the best 'writing tools' available to writers to help bring any story to life.  I love creating dialogue and find that my characters often surprise me as they converse with one another!  I hope you will enjoy writing dialogue as much as I do.

The main functions of dialogue are:

To reveal characters' relationships to each other. *Relationships can be 'shown' rather than 'told,' by what the characters say to one another.*

It can offer information where a character lives, their background and social standing, and what sort of person they are.

Dialogue helps to move the story forwards.  *It enables the reader to visualise what is taking place and to hear the character's voice. Furthermore, it breaks up blocks of narration. Many readers are 'put off' when presented with a dense page of text – I know I am!*

ncrease the tension.  *Drama is created by what is said and how it is said, although what is not said can also add to the tension. Sometimes a character's 'internal thought' can be placed alongside dialogue. Only that of your viewpoint character though! Internal thought will be covered in a later section.*

**Choose one of the scenarios below to practise your dialogue skills, paying attention to how it should be set out**.

At this stage, keep the dialogue between just two characters. Hopefully, you can choose a scenario you can use in your life story.

1. One character has taken something belonging to the other.
2. Two characters are reuniting after not seeing one another for some time.
3. One character is giving another some bad news.
4. A character is trying to get out of something they don't want to do.
5. Two characters are planning something.
6. A character is saying goodbye to the other.

**Approach the task as follows:**

1. Start by using only spoken words. [cwb5.1]
2. Re-write, adding character action or speech tags to show who is speaking. [cwb5.2]
3. Read the speech aloud to check authenticity.

**'Rules' when writing dialogue**

1. New speaker – new line.
2. Speech marks go on the outside of punctuation marks.
3. Try not to overuse speech tags. (replied, asked, said, etc.)
4. Use character action to break up the dialogue. *You can show anger, excitement, etc by what a character does and how they do it. (e.g. Sarah*

16

*slammed the book onto the table. "I can't do it!")*

5. Go easy on the adverbs, (Happily, slowly, etc)
6. Read your dialogue aloud to check it flows.

Creating conversations between characters is one of the most exciting aspects of being a writer. Writing is obviously a solitary activity, but you're never lonely when you're immersed in the dialogue of your book!

Don't expect to remember past conversations word for word – don't forget, your life story is <u>your</u> take on something. Recall things from your perspective.

Clearly, if a family member was to be asked to remember something from your past, their viewpoint could alter significantly. But this is your book, not theirs. A certain amount of artistic and authorial licence is permitted.

# Planning Your Book

This section will help you plan your life story out in more depth and bring together the pieces you have written so far.

Some writers claim not to plan anything and be able to launch straight into their writing. I think a plan can only be helpful, so I advocate at least *trying* the planning strategies I offer.

If you have a structure to follow, you are more likely to achieve completion. Having only a skeleton outline of your story ensures there is less likelihood of you stalling along the way, as you always have your plan to refer back to. So let's start by looking at your story as a whole.

[cwb6.1] **Complete the following *where, when, who, what, why* prompts.** These bring together some of the writing elements you have considered so far and will reaffirm why you are doing what you are doing, and undertaking this writing project.

**Where?** – *Where are the main settings? Refer to the section on setting. You could also list other settings that you have now identified to use in your story*

**When?** – *What period will your story cover? Exactly when does it start and finish? Are there any cultural references you could include to show the era*

(For example, music, cars, politics, fashions, etc.)

**Who?** - *Give the names of the main characters here – are you going to change any names from real life?* This decision can cause difficulties – in an ideal world you would gain permission from anyone included in your book. If you feel using real names could lead to defamation allegations, or you are dealing with sensitive issues, you ought to consider changing names and basic details to protect identities – this is what I did in my memoir, 'Don't Call me Mum.' You could also write under a pen name.

**What?** *This is the difficult part! Can you give a brief outline of your **plot** in two or three sentences? Imagine someone stops you in the street and asks, 'what is your book about?'*

**Why?** *What is going to be different about your book? Why are you writing it? Who are you writing it for? What is special about it? You must keep this in mind at all stages! It will keep you going through the trickier parts and if you are stalling.*

Next, we shall increase the potential content of your book.

[cwb6.2] **Make lists of relevant, significant events** that have oc-curred in your life, and you want to write about. They must fall between the start and end points of your story or memoir, identified in the above task. Only choose significant events that you want to include in your story. For example:

- Births, deaths, marriages. (*You might want to write these under three separate headings.*)
- Moves; house, job, study. (*Again, you might want to work under three separate headings.*)

- New and old relationships. (*Romantic, friendship, family, work.*)
- Endings of things. *(E.g. holidays, eras.)*
- 'Firsts.' *(E.g. first love, first day at school, first job, first time abroad.)*
- Any other general, but memorable, and perhaps life-changing events.

Don't expect to remember everything! You can keep adding as things come to mind. There will, of course, be some overlap in what you have written.

[cwb6.3] **Keep adding to your lists** – apply dates if you can, (even if they are just rough ideas of the approximate year,) to each occurrence.

# Scene Planning Techniques

When it comes to writers, there are two types, the 'plotter' and the 'pantser.' The plotter, as the name suggests, plans the minutiae of what they will write before they start, and the pantser flies by the seat of their pants and writes into the dark. I think I fall somewhere between the two and you will find your own way too, as your writing journey progresses.

I am a huge believer in at least some planning which is why I have devoted two sections of this book to planning. Unless you're a pantser, you'll find out how much planning suits you.

Below are five strategies you can use to plan individual scenes prior to writing them. You should find that your writing flows easily when you have an idea of what will be contained within each scene, and where it is heading.

## 1. [cwb7.1] Bullet pointing

This is the easiest strategy. Write a bullet pointed series of words or phrases that will guide you through the progression of a scene or chapter. This is useful when leaving a longer piece of work for the day.

For example:

- Mark arrives back home with his daughter
- They look around the house for Lauren
- He tries to contact her, etc.

## 2. [cwb7.2] **Who, What, When, Where and Why?**

- **Who** are your characters? Who will be in the scene?
- **What** will happen in your scene? Something must happen in the scene that is moving the story forward.
- **When** will it be set? Time of day, year, era, etc.
- **Where?** Where will it be set?
- **Why** must it be written? If you can't answer this, the scene probably should be omitted from your book. Every single scene must do a job or 'singing for its supper,' as I always say in my face-to-face courses.

## 3. [cwb7.3] **Planning through the senses**

In the scene you are about to write, what will be seen, heard, smelt tasted and felt?

These details will increase reader connection to your story.

## 4. [cwb7.4] **Scene Progression**

- Scene Introduction:
- Next:
- Then:
- Conclusion:

**5.** [cwb7.5] **Plotting a Story Arc** Scenes, chapters, novels, memoirs and short stories and flash fiction are often 'arc shaped.'

That is, they start with an introduction and then follow a line of rising action, with peaks and troughs, to a climax then back down to a resolution.

You could draw an arc shape and then plot the progression your piece will take.

# What Makes a Good Story Opening?

You have already decided the point at which your story will start. Now you are going to hone it into your book opening, to grab the reader and compel them to read on.

An engaging story opening must embody as many of the following characteristics as possible.

It should:

**Start in the best place:**

Go straight in at a point where something is happening, rather than offering a lot of backstory and description.

I have often chopped pages off the start of a book, realising that I'm stage setting rather than launching in at an action point.

**Introduce the main character:**

Whose story is it? Introduce the main character, (i.e. you!) Ensure there is a reason for emotional connection. You have to make the reader care and create an immediate bond.

**Introduce other main character(s):**

This isn't essential in your opening, but the introduction of other characters can add depth and create intrigue.

**Show the setting:**

Ensure a potential reader of your story can visualise the backdrop for which they are reading. This is best achieved through sensory information.

**Dialogue, thought or action:**

Have your character say, think, or do something – preferably all three. Something must be happening.

**A flavour of what's to come:**

If possible, offer something of the 'crux' of the story. For example, the desire to have a stable home, to break free of something or to find something out.

Make sure you set the tone for the rest of the book in terms of voice. e.g. if your story is going to have a funny or sad edge, give a flavour of this at the beginning.)

**Intrigue:**

The story opening should raise questions that the reader will have to read on to have answered.

You could look at the story openings of the published autobiographies and memoirs you are reading. Consider what you like (or not) about each one of them. Do they make you want to read on? [cwb8.1]

Apply your thoughts to your own story opening, perhaps using one of the planning strategies mentioned in the previous section. Ensure that your opening line is strong enough to hook your potential reader. The rest of the book should keep them hooked, and we're going to look in subsequent sections at how to do that.

[cwb8.2] Write your opening scene in full, ensuring you incorporate as many of the aforementioned aspects as possible, in order to write a great opening scene.

# Writing With Your Reader in Mind

Writing and reading are two sides of the same coin. Once books have been written, edited, and handed over to a reader, they are no longer just the author's words. They now belong with the reader to make of them what they will.

I find it a really exciting prospect that readers take our words to create their own pictures and worlds.

An unwritten contract is formed between author and reader; they will keep reading as long as we provide them with an immersive reading experience. And then hopefully, they will recommend your book to other readers and seek out more of your work.

As mentioned, it is wise to think about <u>who</u> you want to read your story once it has been written. If you write to keep your envisaged readers engaged and interested, you will write a better book.

Knowing who your reader is will also make marketing easier when you get to that stage. Keep the following in mind as you continue to write:

**Readers read for the following reasons:**

- To be entertained.
- To learn something new – to be educated.
- For self-development/to overcome a problem.
- For relaxation.
- For escapism.

**One or more of the following aspects will keep readers turning the pages of an autobiography or memoir:**

- An easy to read, well-written narrative structure, which they can be immersed in.
- Emotional connections with the characters.
- A situation they can relate to – this might include era and cultural references.
- A story and journey they are interested in.
- A desire to know the outcome and how things will turn out.
- Pace and tension.

[cwb9.1] Respond to the following questions to help you think more about your book and its potential readers:

**What is the title of your book?**

*This could be a 'working title' at this stage.*

**What might you have on the cover?**

*Colour, image, font, blurb, endorsement, etc.*

**Who might want to read your story?**

*Age, gender, background, circumstances.*

## Why will they be interested in your book?

*What experience can you promise them?*

## What would you want to say to them before they start reading?

*What experience, information and insight can you promise them?*

## How will you want them to feel *after* reading?

*Remember emotion is the key to reader engagement.*

Hopefully, you are now in the habit of writing at least two scenes every week. These should be taken from the overall planning you completed in the planning section, where you started listing events and occasions that fall within the timeline of your book. And remember to add to your list as and when you recall them.

Keep choosing from this list, writing the scenes you feel most compelled to write on any given day. Use one of the planning approaches previously suggested until you find the one best suited to you.

# The Narrative Elements of Writing

What you are aiming for as a writer is to balance the following components in your writing: setting, back story, character action, interiority, dialogue and emotion.

At the first draft stage, this is difficult and as I've mentioned before, you are best to concentrate on getting the words down and worry about tidying up for your reader later. The typing up and editing stage is the time to keep this balance and interweaving of narrative components in mind.

Below is a short extract showing an interweaving of narrative elements. Read through it once and then go back through it, identifying which is setting, back story, character action, interiority, dialogue and emotion. [cwb10.1]

*"Can we play on the slide Daddy." She wiped her mouth on the back of her glove.*

*"Maybe soon. But first, I need to tell you that I'm going away for a little while." He tucked his wallet back into his pocket.*

*"Where?" Christopher spoke even though his mouth was full of ice-cream. "Can I come?"*

*"I'm afraid not." Dad patted the top of Christopher's hat.*

*"When will you be back? Is it like a holiday? What about Mum? Is she going too?" I fired questions at him, hardly stopping for breath and then took a bite of my flake.*

*"No." Dad laughed, but it was a sad laugh.*

*A dog ran over, wanting some of Joanna's ice-cream. She screamed.*

*"I'm so sorry," said its owner, who had run after it. "Come on Ben. You are a very rude dog."*

*"I'm not sure when I'll be back," Dad continued.*

*"When will we see you again?" My eyes were hot with tears. Grandma had died not long before and now Dad was going away too. It was all too much. I looked at Joanna and Christopher who were sat happily licking their ice-creams. Perhaps they didn't understand what was going on.*

*"I'm not sure love." Dad reached across the picnic table for my gloved hand that didn't have an ice-cream in it, but I snatched it away. A tear slid down my cheek, making it feel warm for a moment.*

Below is another method for planning a scene which helps with the balance of the components that create a successful narrative.

Before you write your next scene, consider and respond to each element as a plan for your own scene. [cwb10.2]

1. **Setting** Where is the scene taking place? This should be brought to life using all the senses.
2. **Back Story** What has gone before, to bring each character to the point they are at now.
3. **Character Action** What are the characters 'doing' as they talk to one another or think something to themselves.
4. **Interiority** What is the character 'thinking.' This should be presented alongside what they are saying or doing. Remember, you can only show what your <u>viewpoint</u> character is thinking. (You

can't read the minds of other characters!!)

5. **Dialogue** Dialogue between characters 'shows' what is happening, rather than just telling.

6. **Emotion** What binds a scene together and what engages a reader is the use of emotion. It enables the reader to feel whatever the main character is feeling.

[10.3] **Now write a scene from this overview**, aiming for a seamless 'interweaving' of these narrative elements as you write.

Keep these principles in mind as you continue working on your book.

# Using Diary Entry to Tell your Story

There is a freedom in writing autobiography and memoir, in that a variety of storytelling approaches can be used to take the narrative forwards. They can be sporadically used throughout your story, at different times.

For example, one chapter might comprise a list, the next might be a flashback, and another, a script. This is the approach I took when I wrote my memoir, 'Don't Call me Mum.'

Your story doesn't have to be told in a linear and wholly narrative way. This section looks at telling your story through the writing of diary entries. This practice is known as *epistolary writing.* (Which also includes the use of writing of letters, emails and text messages – more about letters in the next section.)

Diarising a narrative allows the focus to be on specific and meaningful episodes, leaving out more mundane events, so a reader can fill in gaps themselves. It enables the reader to connect with the narrator and the characters and helps establish and maintain that all-important emotional connection.

Anyone who has ever kept a diary knows that it permits the unleashing of personal thoughts and secrets, even more so because the expectation is that no one else will ever read what we have written. This further increases that aforementioned emotional attachment.

This process does not have to be 'day after day.' Weeks, months or even years can elapse between diary entries. There can be a variation in length, tone and content of each entry, as there would be in a real diary. Entries can be given further depth by being broken down into times.

For example:

*5.36 There is no point in just laying here. I might as well get up. Feeling terrified about what is ahead today.*

*6.04 No point trying to eat anything. Can't.*

*8.30 Hairdresser has arrived. Starting to look more presentable.*

An entire story can be told in this way or just a section of it. It offers a really unique dimension.

[11.1] **Choose a scene/event from your overall plan which you could take forward using this diarising method.** Start before the event – as far as is necessary to effectively anticipate and convey the scene. (You may know the exact date.)

Write a diary entry as though you are writing on that date. Make sure you include a recount of one or more things that are going on, how you are feeling and who else is involved.

Continue with the day of the actual event. Keep going with as many days as is necessary to complete the process of conveying what you experienced. Remember, this does not have to be 'day after day.' Week, months or even years can elapse between diary entries.

There can be a variation in length, tone and content of each entry. As there would be in a diary kept in real life.

# Using Letters to Tell Your Story

In the last section, you were introduced to the practice of epistolary writing and it focused on moving an event in your life forward with diary entries. In this section you will see how the use of letters can give your autobiography or memoir added interest.

There are other epistolary writing techniques you can use, such as lists, transcripts of conversations, emails and text messages. Your story does not have to be told in a solely 'narrative' way.

Because I wrote my own memoir in this way and the feedback from readers has been great, I can advocate it. Apparently, using all these techniques for storytelling offers a more interesting and a page-turning experience.

A diary is you, communicating with yourself, (through the page.) You are now going to take the same approach, but as the writer of *letters* which involves you communicating with *others* as a device for moving your story forward.

**Make a list of specific times in your life where communication by letter has happened. For example:** [cwb12.1]

- A friend who moved away.
- A relative working away.
- Someone serving in the forces.
- A child studying away.
- You, on an extended break somewhere.
- A legal situation.
- An exchange of 'love letters.'

[cwb12.2] **Choose one exchange** to write about – this could be a standalone letter or a series of letters, relevant in your life story and will help to move it forward.

Dates do not have to be exact, but still necessary to give the letters an idea of the era. It needs to be clear who the senders and receivers are.

Be sure to include emotion to keep your reader engaged, as well as some contextual information where possible. (Era, setting other characters, backstory and future plans.) You will find it helpful to plan this before writing, unless you're a pantser!

The letters need not be exact. You will be cherry-picking the information that will take your story forward, whilst holding the interest of your readers.

I hope you will find this way of writing as liberating as I do. We are writing in an era where anything goes in terms of structure and the more unique we can be, the more chance we have of standing out amongst other autobiographical writers.

# Show, Don't Tell

*Show, don't tell* is a technique used in all types of writing. It enables readers to experience a narrative through character action, sensory language, dialogue, description and thoughts.

The reader is given the opportunity to interpret details in the text themselves, rather than being *told* everything. It makes reading a more active and therefore, a more enjoyable process.

Where an author does this well, the reader can be in the moment, feeling and experiencing events alongside characters. A balance of showing and telling ensures a stronger story.

Below are five examples of how to show, not tell.

**Using Character Action**

*I stood for a while, staring at the door. I could literally feel my heart pumping. Finally, I knocked.*

*What we can infer:* Character apprehension is shown through how the character is acting. It is not necessary to say 'she was scared.'

## Using Sensory Language

*The smell took me right back. It was the aftershave he'd worn when we'd been dating. When things were different.*

*What we can infer:* In this instance, smell conveys nostalgia. 'She missed him' is not needed.

## Using Dialogue

*I bellowed after his retreating form.* "Get back here this instant!"

*What we can infer:* That the character is angry.

## Using Description

*I cradled my notebook in my arms like a lover. Together, we had created history.*

*What we can infer:* That the character is proud of something that has been written is obvious.

## Using Internal Thought

It's fine, honestly." I folded my arms. *You'll get what's coming to you...*

*What we can infer:* The character is planning something and things are not fine. We are shown, rather than told.

cwb13.1] **Write a scene, using each of the methods of 'showing, not telling,' to write an episode from your life. (e.g. action, speech,**

**description, thought and sensory description.)**

## Character Action

Choose a time you have felt a particular emotion. (E.g. excited, nervous, scared,) and show it through how you were *acting*.

## Sensory Language

Choose one or more of the senses to describe how you have felt about a memory. (e.g. smelling something familiar, hearing a particular song) Show how you felt through the language you use to recollect.

## Dialogue

Write a verbal exchange between yourself and another character to show how you have felt about something at a point in time, without actually telling. (E.g. grateful, jealous, angry)

## Description

Through your description of an object, show how you felt about it (Something you cherished or something you wanted rid of.)

## Internal Thought

Through what you were thinking towards something or someone, show how you were secretly feeling.

As you continue writing scenes for your life story, keep the above methods in your mind as you write. Once the writing has gone 'cold and you revisit it to edit, that is a good time to ask yourself whether you have shown, rather than told.

# Don't Get Stuck – Keep Your Momentum

We will now address two key aspects of dealing with the point you are at now as a writer – the first is your confidence, and the second is ensuring you keep the momentum with your story.

Writing is a solitary activity and many writers lack confidence in their work at times, particularly when the writing isn't flowing all that well.

It is vitally important you keep that self-belief and excitement in your writing, after all, if *you* don't believe in what you are doing, neither will potential publishers or readers. Your story is unique and deserves its place on bookshop shelves amongst the others. Never lose sight of that

We all have days where we struggle to write or days when we wonder who on earth will want to ever read what we have written – I have had many. The best thing we can do is accept the wobble, and get back on with our writing.

Writing is an industry where rejection can be a common occurrence therefore positive self-talk can be a valuable tool to stave off self-doubt and the fear of failure.

An affirmation is a positive phrase, (written in first person, presen tense) stating a goal or a truth that you want to impress into your mind.

The theory is that by clearing your mind and repeating this phrase to yourself out loud and invoking positive emotions of determination, peace and your joy of writing, you can create this belief in your conscious mind. A writer might use an affirmation like, *"I am creative and talented."* It might sound a bit woo-woo but honestly it works!

## How Writers Use Affirmations

1. Keep them brief and specific. They will be easier to incorporate into your mind.
2. Use the present tense. Instead of *"By next year, I will be famous,"* focus on *today. "I have a special gift with words." Or "I can write anything."*
3. Choose a realistic affirmation. Instead of *"I am a best-selling author."* Try *"I am moving toward my goal of writing a great autobiography."*
4. Say your affirmation to yourself routinely. When you wake up or before you go to sleep and feel those positive emotions.
5. Write down your affirmation. [cwb14.1] You can post it on your computer, stick it on the bathroom mirror, or carry it with you. The act of writing it down and seeing it in print will help fix it in your mind and invoke those positive emotions.

**Here are examples of positive affirmations you could use:**

1. *I am a writer. Writing is my art.*
2. *My wonderful memoir will not write itself.*
3. *I am creative. My words flow easily.*
4. *I write every day and love doing it.*
5. *I can visualise success, and I have the patience and talent to reach it.*

6. *I can be a successful writer.*
7. *No one else can write this autobiography, but me.*
8. *People will want to read my interesting and exciting story.*

Writing an autobiography or memoir requires commitment and self-discipline. There may be times when you find it impossible to devote the hours you need or find the energy for your writing. Here are some ideas to keep you moving forward:

## Work on your story every day

Even if you only write notes, or think about it. Set a goal such as writing a page a day or spending half an hour a day. You will then have evidence of progress.

## Keep Reading

Not only for pleasure, but as part of your writing education. Mark passages you like or dislike - try to figure out why they make you feel the way you do.

Pay attention to how other authors combine dialogue and narration, the effect of the vocabulary they choose, and the way they have structured their scenes into chapters.

## Appoint a particular time of day (or night) to write

Make it a habit you want to keep. Writing needs regular practice. If you schedule your writing time – the way you would an appointment, you are giving your writing the priority it deserves.

## How to Find more Time.

*It's hard to find time to write*, is what everybody says. There are always so many other things that need to be done. The truth is, you probably won't *find* the time to write; so you will have to *make* the time:

- Get up an hour earlier, make a coffee and start writing.
- Use your journey to work to write on the train or listen to an audio book in the car.
- Write during your lunch hour.
- Decide that an hour of writing time is more important than an hour of television.

What change can you make to your routine to afford more writing time? [cwb14.2]

*Thinking* is also an important part of the writing process. If you've established your regular daily writing time, make the most of that time by preparing yourself mentally beforehand. My best ideas seem to come when I'm swimming or doing the ironing, so start thinking about your story when you're washing the dishes or walking the dog so that, when you sit down to write, you are ready to write. If you can't set aside time every day to write, you could be thinking about where you're going next in your writing.

By thinking about your story even when you aren't writing it, you'll make it a natural and necessary part of your life, and it all counts as time and effort spent on your book.

## A Place of Your Own

You need a *place* as your writing space, where you won't be interrupted. Ideally, where you can leave your work out when you're finished for the day. Space for your computer and printer, and plenty of desktop space to spread out your notes and other materials. A noticeboard, where you can pin up inspirational quotes, pictures of settings and characters, deadlines, etc. is a great addition to your writing space.

Make sure you have adequate lighting, a comfortable chair and a shelf for reference books. Create a place that is your own and what others come to know is your own special writing place. If it is really impossible to carve out a place, then have a portable tray to keep all your writing things together.

What changes can you make to improve your writing space? [cwb14.3]

Make the most of whatever time and space you have. Writers work in cafes, on buses and trains. Any place is a good place to write. For most a quiet place is ideal, for others music is essential, and it is possible to turn out good writing in the middle of total chaos. When my children were small, I've been known to write in a soft-play area!

## Re-Starter System

No matter what you accomplish, you'll often have to pick up in the middle of something left unfinished, and you may be worried about picking up the thread of your thoughts in the next session.

Ernest Hemingway used to stop in the middle of a well-thought-out scene; stopping writing whilst still flowing. When he was eager to go on to the next word—when he knew *exactly* what he wanted to say—that's when he'd stop for the day, often in the middle of a sentence.

Hemingway seldom had trouble getting started the following day. He knew the rest of the sentence he'd left hanging; and where he wanted the story to go next.

This is something I've tried and it definitely works but what works even better, is briefly bullet pointing where I want to go next.

# Pace

Pace plays a vitally important role in our writing. When used well, we can keep readers on the edge of their seat before being offered a reprieve. Pacing almost always determines the reader's level of engagement with a story. Fast-paced books are often described as 'page turners,' and as writers, that is exactly what we should aspire to.

**Definition of Pace**

Narrative pace determines how quickly or how slowly the writer takes a reader through a story. It relies on a combination of mood and emotion, as these elements play out in the dialogue, setting and action. For example, Michelle Obama's "Becoming" has a faster pace than Elizabeth Gilbert's "Eat, Pray, Love."

The pace of a story can vary, for example, the opening pace may feel different from that of the story's ending.

**Upping the Pace**

Fast action and rapid sequencing increase the pace. Action sequences containing little dialogue and minimal internal character thought best create fast action. Rapid sequencing is where moments happen one right after the other, helping the pace of the story feel faster. Where dialogue is used, it should be 'short and snappy,' not interwoven with too much thought and detail.

**Slowing It Down**

Narrative passages that contain more detail, establishing setting and containing longer sentences, feel slower. This helps build suspense and allows the reader to catch their breath between action sequences. Where dialogue is used, it can be more detailed and accompanied with character thought and setting description.

**Striking a Balance**

The most interesting stories contain scenes that move at different speeds. They keep the reader engaged. Placing chapters or scenes side by side that feature description, thought and emotion, alongside those with fast-paced action sequences can strike the right balance.

cwb15.1] **Write a scene in which you are travelling to a destination. Write at a *fast* pace.**

- Words with fewer syllables.
- Strong verbs – e.g. swing, march, drag.
- Minimal dialogue and internal thought.
- Short sentences.
- Action rather than description.

cwb15.2] **Now write a scene in which you leave that destination. Write at a *slow* pace.**

- Longer sentences.
- Scene setting.
- Description.
  Internal thoughts.
- More expression of emotion.
- Soft verbs – e.g. tuck, tug, fumble.

Through this exercise, also focus on allowing your reader to infer from the journey, what takes place whilst you are at the destination.

# Tension

The ability to portray tension is a vital tool in your 'writer's toolbox.' It creates the drama that will keep your readers enthralled. In narrative terms, it means: *How the writer 'holds back' what the character wants.*

## 1. Set up the tension

Your story should keep saying *no* to your main character. Whatever has been wanted or needed should be held back. The best conflict is one that appears insurmountable, so pile on the difficulties. To increase tension, we should not make situations easier; always harder. So in terms of life story, try to show your reader what obstacles have been placed in your way and how you have overcome them.

To really increase the tension, ask yourself, "What have been the worst things that have got in the way?"

## 2. Make the reader feel emotion

Use internal conflict to its best advantage: abandonment, mistrust, emotional deprivation, dependence, social exclusion, or another vulnerability. You can use those conflicts and flaws to challenge readers to keep reading and to keep them caring. If you as the writer can feel the emotion, you can convey it effectively to the reader.

It doesn't matter what kind of book you are writing or who your characters are—*a story is feelings*. The more that is at stake, the more emotion can be created. The more tragic a character appears, the more tension a reader feels on their behalf, and the more a reader cares for them. Internal and external conflict must be in place to create tension.

### 3. Backstory reduces the tension as it provides answers

Leaving details about what has gone before until later in the story is an effective way to intrigue your readers. Don't fill in all the answers, just give them enough so they won't be frustrated. Backstory in a tense scene slows the pace and reduces tension as it allows the reader a 'breather.' If you must reveal information, you can do it through a quick flash of internal thought or a secondary character's dialogue. Hint at certain details to make the reader want to know more.

Change is what keeps the reader turning pages. New challenges, new information, new twists, and added complications—all ensure extra potential for tension.

[cwb16.1] **Decide what is the over-riding source of tension in *your* story? For example:**

- A quest for a happy family.
- Answers to a problem.
- Help from a particular source.
- To discover the truth, etc.

[cwb16.2] **Then make a list of all the elements in the way of tha**

## objective

Think of a time when you have felt vulnerable in some way. (e.g. distrustful, abandoned, rejected, excluded, etc.) Relive the episode through your writing, ensuring that you include some 'feeling' to enable a reader to feel the emotion alongside you.

Write more scenes from your 'skeleton plan,' keeping your story's over-riding tension in mind as you continue to write. Have your readers 'rooting' for you as the main character.

Ensure you are keeping all your pieces organised and listing what you have written and keeping it all in date order. If you are typing work up, keep it all in one document and in order.

As more scenes or events occur to you, that you know you want to include, add them to your skeleton plan to remain aware of what still needs to be written.

# Point of View

As the writer of an autobiography or memoir, you will probably be writing in first-person viewpoint. However, this is not always the case I wrote my own memoir in third person for two reasons. First, because it was emotive content and a third person viewpoint disconnected me from it. Second, writing in third person allows the reader to make it more 'their' story.

It is useful for you to know which points of view are available to you as a writer, and to experiment with them. Viewpoint is determined by how a character has the camera on them. It will be first, second, third multiple or omniscient.

It is helpful to take a 'cinematic' approach as the writer, that is, to imagine the scenes are being acted out on set. I give more explanation for each below:

## 1st Person (I/me)

Where the 'camera' looks through the eyes of a single character.

**Advantage:** This creates immediacy and intimacy with the reader and involves them more directly. This viewpoint can be shifted around characters, as long as it is clear when it is being changed.

**Disadvantage:** Nothing can happen without the viewpoint character. This can be restrictive.

**Example:** I didn't feel too bad to say I had hardly slept all night. I had chosen my outfit carefully. Something similar to what Sally would wear – a pinafore dress. I felt quite nice in that. I hoped no one would notice my shoes. A hand-me-down from my cousin.

## 2nd Person (you)

Where the narrator/character addresses either the reader directly, or another character in the story as though they are listening/reading. It is a lesser used viewpoint but can be effective and engaging if done well and consistently. The narrator/character still has the camera behind their eyes, but they're pointing it directly at the reader.

**Example:** *You're uncharacteristically early and the first person I notice when I step through the heavy wooden doors, fifteen minutes before the service is due to begin.*

*I want to shout at you when I see what you're wearing. Trackies. Hoodie. Trainers. You never did have any respect for her, did you?*

## Third Person (single viewpoint) (he/she)

Technically, the same as first person; the main difference is in the pronoun and the fact that the effect is less intimate and confessional. As in first person, this viewpoint can be shifted as long as it is clear when it is being changed. The narrator still has the camera, but instead of it being behind their eyes, it's as though it's being carried on their shoulder.

**Advantage:** Immediacy and intimacy is created with the reader, however there is more distance than when using first person.

**Disadvantage:** Nothing can happen without the viewpoint character. This can be restrictive.

**Example:** *"It would have been quicker to walk." Ellen dug her fingers into her bag and sat forwards. "Excuse me," she muttered to the lady next to her.*
*"You can't get off here," the driver said. "We're at the lights."*
*"Watch me." Ellen pressed the emergency exit button and jumped onto the pavement, breaking into a run as her kitten heels made contact with the concrete.*

### Third Person (multiple viewpoint) (he/she)

Viewpoint shifts from character to character. The reader is privy to the thoughts of all characters but with no authorial knowledge outside of what the characters have. It is wise to limit the number of viewpoints used and to make it clear when the viewpoint changes. Usually a change of scene is used for each viewpoint change. It is as though the camera is being passed from character to character.

**Advantage:** it is easier for the author to tell the story.

**Disadvantage:** it is harder for the reader to become emotionally involved with a particular character and can be confusing.

**Example:** *They stride away from the renewed frenzy, amidst further flashing bulbs. Paul feels an unfamiliar jauntiness to his step for the firs* *time in a long time.He never has to see that place again.*

*"He's been acquitted. He's sat here with his first pint. Why don't you come over?" Alana speaks guardedly into her phone to Lee, not wanting Paul to hear. "It looks bad that you don't appear to have taken an interest and you won't wish him well."*

*"Nah you're alright." It's the last place Lee wants to be. He can't pretend he's happy with how things have turned out.*

## Omniscient Narrator or 'God's Eye View'

An 'all-seeing, all-knowing' narrative view where the viewpoint not only shifts from character to character but into the narration as well. This enables general overviews to be provided or the possibility of going off on digressionary asides, but then to zoom back in close. It is as though the camera is up in the air, above the 'stage.'

**Advantage:** it is versatile and flexible in terms of storytelling and conveying information.

**Disadvantage:** it distances the reader from identification with the characters as it is an objective and impersonal viewpoint. It is little used in contemporary fiction and regarded as quite old-fashioned now.

**Example:** *"Why are you sleeping here Daddy?" Emily was surprised to find her father asleep on the sofa.*

*"Ssssh, sweetheart. Mummy's sleeping." Paul yawned as he sat up. "We don't want to wake her up." It didn't feel like five minutes since he's fallen asleep. He felt exhausted.*

*"Can I open the curtains Daddy?" She bounced towards the window. "Let the sunshine in?" She liked it when it was just her and her dad. Their neighbour, happy to see Emily, smiled at her from the garden next door.*

*Paul's heart felt like a melon within him. It would take more than an open curtain to enable him to feel some sunshine.*

*"Can you get me some breakfast Daddy?" She flung the door of the living room open as she spoke, forgetting that she was supposed to be keeping quiet.*

*Michelle jumped out of bed, angry that they had woken her up. "For God's sake!"*

As an autobiographical writer, you will probably write using the pronouns I/me/my.

[cwb17.1] However, you may like to experiment with the pronoun, and write a section of your narrative viewpoint in third person (he/she/they/character names.)

Consider the effect it has. You may notice that writing in third person creates a distance between character and reader. This can be good if you're working with really sensitive content.

[cwb17.2] Now try writing in second person viewpoint. (You/your/name) Remember, you are addressing another character who isn't there or the reader directly. Try this for the duration of a scene.

# Voice

By now you will hopefully be amassing a considerable body of writing. Be sure to keep each scene and anecdote indexed, dated and in order amongst the rest of your work.

It is difficult to write a life story chronologically as memories will occur to you sporadically and everyday conversations will take place, evoking memories of events you may want to include.

In addition, each writing skill you are working on and experimenting with throughout the course will evoke writing, but not necessarily in any sort of orderly sequence. I hope that all makes sense!

In the last section, we looked at viewpoint, and this closely aligns with voice, although there is a distinction between the two. Voice is determined by the choice of character to tell the story and how his choice 'colours' the way it is told. Aspects such as the character's personality, backstory, accent, experience, etc, inform its telling, whereas viewpoint refers to the lens we choose to tell it through.

An early decision we need to make as writers is *who do I want the reader to connect with?* For example, we could write a memoir mainly about a family member, so we may wish to use their voice either for the entire duration of the book or for an occasional chapter of it. This multi-voice approach can add depth, providing the voices are distinctive from one another.

The language used is also very important – their words, phrases, accent and slang need to be consistent throughout. This choice of character voice can make a marked difference to the progression and tone of a story, so it is important to make the right choices.

[cwb18.1] **Ask yourself as you continue:**

- What emotional aspects can the reader connect to with the main character?
- What will make the reader care about the viewpoint character?
- Is the main character's voice distinct from that of other characters in the story?
- Is the way they speak and think relatable?
- Is their voice consistent throughout the story?

[cwb18.2] **Re-write a scene from your autobiography, considering the effect when you change the voice within the scene.**

So, take an event or incident you have written in your voice and tell it in the voice of another character who was there. Stay in the same viewpoint though (e.g. I/me/my)

# Tense

The tense you write in can have a huge effect on your story. It is worth experimenting to see whether swapping tense can improve your story.

Unsurprisingly, the most common tense used in autobiographies and memoirs is past tense – however present tense can offer a unique edge for your story if you enjoy using it.

Examples of past and present tense are given below.

## Past

To tell a story in past tense is more usual than other tenses, relating back to the days of verbal storytelling. A story can be given authenticity if told as though it has happened, especially in the autobiographical genre.

### Example

No, I won't. I don't look at your bloody phone." He reached for the kitchen door handle. "If you don't trust me, it's your problem." She lunged at the pocket he was guarding with his other hand. "Get off me!" She grasped his arm. Her nails dug into it. "You're hurting me!"

**Present**

It gives a sense of immediacy and increases the closeness between the reader and the story in that they feel they are experiencing the action as it is unfolding. You can also use present tense to write about how you feel about past events.

**Example**

*"No, I won't. I don't look at your bloody phone." He reaches for the kitchen door handle. "If you don't trust me, it's your problem." She lunges at the pocket he is guarding with his other hand. "Get off me!" She grasps his arm Her nails dig into it. "You're hurting me!"*

[cwb19.1] Re-write a scene from your autobiography, considering the effect when you change the tense of the story.

For example, if you have written in past tense, try changing it into present. ('I turned away from him and walked away' becomes 'I turn away from him and walk away.')

Or vice versa. ('She looks at me in a way that makes me uncomfortable' becomes, 'she looked at me in a way which made me uncomfortable.')

It can have a remarkable effect and at this stage, if you were to change your tense throughout your book, it wouldn't be too great a task.

# Tightening Your Writing

Editing is an essential part of writing. It can be likened to polishing a precious jewel until it shines. A piece of writing is never truly finished, more a point is reached where it can be left.

This section will look at paring your work down, and the next section will focus *on* improving and expanding it.

Normally, you should not edit anything until your entire first draft is complete, but for the sake of continuing to build your writing skills throughout the course, editing is something that will be considered now. I love the editing stage, but obviously you need a solid first draft before you can embark on it.

Unnecessary words and phrases can easily find their way into our writing and drag it down. Writing should be as concise, yet as meaningful as possible.

*Eliminate superfluous words* Make a list of these. The words you throw in out of habit like *quite, really, very* and *just.* Or phrases like *began to* or *started to.* My biggest culprits that I have to eliminate are *a little* and *a bit.*

***Avoid being too wordy.*** Don't use four words when two will say the same thing. (Grey and cloudy sky – *overcast sky.* Don't use an adverb when you can use a stronger verb. (She cuddled the baby tightly - *she clasped him to her.)* If two adjectives are similar, pick the best one and lose the other. (…trying to listen through the solid, heavy door – *solid door.)*

Print a random page of your book and weed out at one word from every sentence. It may not be possible, but it's a valuable exercise. If a word doesn't add importance to a sentence, it should go. Do this throughout your story – a sentence at a time.

***Lose speech tags.*** You should definitely have dialogue in your story – it is one of the biggest things that brings it to life. If the reader knows who is speaking, you don't need to keep telling them — especially in a scene with only two characters.

And remove all those flowery verbs that stick out, such as *quizzed, extrapolated, exclaimed*, and *interjected*. They can 'jar' a reader out of a story. Just use *said* and *asked*, and maybe an occasional *replied* or *answered*.

***Search and get rid of repetition.*** We often repeat words, phrases, or ideas in the same paragraph.

***And a word about backstory*** Look at all the incidences of backstory and reduce to a few lines of the most important information that the reader *must* know to "get" the story.

Can a character *think* or *say* these things instead of going into a lengthy description?

[cwb 20.1] **Choose an earlier piece of first draft writing (one scene)** and apply the suggestions offered above. Deal with one sentence at a time.

**Carry on the above process until you have a complete chapter edited in this way**. You will work with this in the next section.

Keep drafting scenes from your 'planning list' that still need to be written.

# Editing and Proofreading Your Work

In the last section, you began the process of tightening a section of your life story and removing some of the 'bloat' from it. I hope you are seeing the difference this makes.

In this section, the reverse will be implemented; improving what you have already, and adding in bits that have been skipped over.

As I've said before, the editing process should not usually be carried out when drafting your work. (But for skill development purposes, this rule needs to be broken.)

Generally, you should get your story and thoughts and ideas down first. And there is no need to concentrate on spelling, layout or punctuation until you get to the final editing stage.

Use this checklist when editing – a scene of your story at a time:

- Decide whether your chapter, scene, or anecdote has started in the right place. Writers often launch in too early, giving too much explanation or backstory first rather than going straight in at point of action.
- Editing means not only 'cutting' things – bits that you've 'skipped

over' may need expansion and events may need to be added.
- Check every word is the best it can be. Use a thesaurus to help. Or the 'synonyms' function on your computer. Every word counts.
- Ensure consistency of viewpoint, character details, etc.
- Remember that reading should be an active process – enable the reader to 'fill in gaps' themselves and infer information.
- Wherever possible, showing rather than tell.
- Know what your piece is trying to achieve, its message, its journey. Has it been successful in doing this?

Below are three essential editing processes that all my work undergoes and yours will need to as well.

1. Print your work out and annotate with a pen. You will notice things on the page you haven't on the screen.
2. Read it aloud – this highlights any issues with flow, especially your dialogue, and will show up repetition of words and phrases.
3. Get someone else to read it. Another pair of eyes will spot mistakes and they can comment on content.

**Here is an example of an underwritten scene, in bold are suggestions of how it could be improved:**

*It was a lovely sunny day but something was definitely brewing. He had been in a bad mood before he went out and now she was trying to keep busy before his return.*

**How did he show he was in a bad mood?  What is she doing to keep busy?**

*She'd already been on the phone to her friend who had invited her to get out of the way and stay with her but she had thought that she had better stay and face the music.*

**What exactly was said between her and the friend? What might 'facing the music' look like?**

*She found herself remembering all the things that had been happening lately and this just made her more anxious.*

**What things had been happening lately? How does the anxiety manifest itself?**

*Finally, he came back and they had a massive argument. She ended up having to sleep in the spare room.*

**What exactly was said throughout the argument?**

**[cwb 21.1] Re-write the above scene, taking the emboldened suggestions into account.**

**Using the chapter you 'tightened' in the last section, look at one paragraph at a time, checking everything has been fleshed out as much as it can be.**

If any scenes or paragraphs need to be written in, write them out in longhand on the reverse of your typed sheets.

Below is the process I use to write and edit my own writing. As you become more established, you will find your own way, but mine might provide you with a solid framework to start with.

1. Notes and planning of scene/story.
2. First draft (the best bit, in my opinion!) – by hand.
3. Going back over this draft (tightening up) as in the last session.
4. Typing up – improving throughout. This could mean taking bits out or adding things in. Printing out.
5. Going back over this work and improving again (using the attached checklist.)
6. Printing out and annotating with a pen.
7. Taking these amendments back to the computer.
8. Reading aloud.
9. Final proof read.

I realise that's quite a process, but a necessary and rewarding one!

# Setting Yourself Writing Goals/Targets

As you approach the latter part of the course, you have gained a wealth of writing skills and are developing substantially as a writer.

You are now going to reflect on what you have learned, as well as any areas you feel you could develop.

[cwb22.1] Respond to the prompts below, making notes on your strengths and weaknesses in the suggested areas:

**Getting to know a character before you bring them to the page**
*Being able to visualise them, hear their voices and know exactly what they want will make them more realistic to the reader. Are they multi-dimensional?*

**Bringing a setting to life**. *Taking a multi-sensory approach and creating an authentic atmosphere.*

**Dialogue.** *Confidently using it to its full effect to portray how characters relate to one another.*

**Having planning strategies which support and organise you**
*Treating your overall plan as a working document. Employing other planning methods ahead of writing scenes and chapters.*

**Writing with your Reader in mind.** *Being aware of your reader, allowing them to fill in some of the gaps for themselves.*

**First Drafting.** *Having a routine for getting the words down and resisting the urge to keep editing them as you go forward.*

**Epistolic Writing.** *Using a letter writing or diary entry method to move your story along.*

**Show, Don't Tell.** *Showing the reader what is going on, rather than telling. Allowing them to do some of the 'work.'*

**Varying the Pace.** *Knowing how to speed up or slow down the speed at which you take the reader through the story.*

**Creating Tension.** *Knowing how to increase tension so it keeps readers engaged.*

**Viewpoint.** *Being aware of the difference between first, second and third person narration. Staying consistent.*

**Narrative Tense**. *Being aware of the differences between past and present narration and its effects.*

**Editing.** *Knowing how to use a variety of editing techniques to improve your own work.*

**Reading.** *Are you reading other autobiographies? Doing so will improve your writing considerably.*

**If there are any areas you are concerned about, re-read the sec-**

tion notes and re-do the set exercise, (with a new scene.)

**Goal setting may now help you focus on what is still to be done to get to the end of the first draft of your book.**

[cwb22.2] The prompts below will support you in this process:

- How much (%) of your autobiography/memoir have your written? (The first draft.)
- Do you have a clear plan of what still needs to be done?
- What regular time can you give yourself to carry on?

[cwb22.3] **Now set yourself some goals. They should be S.M.A.R.T (Specific, Measurable, Attainable, Realistic, Timed)**

- In the next week, I will –
- In the next month, I will –
- In three months time, I will –
- In six months time, I will –

**Read these goals aloud, display them prominently, and revisit them often.**

**Keep going – you're doing brilliantly!**

# Writing a Synopsis

In this session you will be summarising your book in order to 'sell it' to a prospective publisher or agent, should you decide to follow the traditional publishing route.

This document is known as a 'synopsis.' It forms a vital part of your submission package and accompanies the cover letter, which we will look at in the next section. The submission package will also contain the first three chapters of your book.

It can be difficult to summarise your book in 500-750 words - this is normally what the publisher specifies. It may help if you carry out this task using your skeleton plan, to help you pick out the key points of your book, that is, the backbone on which your story rests.

A synopsis is not to be confused with the blurb; a synopsis is a document that includes the ending and sells the story to an agent or publisher, whereas the blurb is the paragraph on the back cover which will sell your book to a prospective reader.

Feedback I have been given from writers taking my classroom course, has said that they find the process of writing a synopsis, a challenging yet rewarding one. It can help to provide direction and focus, whilst capturing the essence and uniqueness of the story you are offering.

Below, I have offered a checklist which you should refer to before, during and after the writing of your synopsis.

Publishers and literary agents are inundated with submissions, so it's vitally important not to give them any reason to reject you on presentational grounds.

**A synopsis should:**

1. Offer a clear idea of the theme and genre of the book.
2. Suggest who might want to read it. You could suggest other comparable authors or the demographic of potential readers.
3. Use the first sentence as a hook.
4. Start with the main character and whatever they are facing, or trying to overcome, or achieve.
5. Be around 750 words. Be aware, this is harder than it first appears.
6. Be single spaced with numbered pages.
7. Include your name and the book's title (in italics) on each page in the header.
8. Include the genre, (autobiography or memoir,) and the approximate word count on the first page.
9. Give a broad outline summary of the <u>whole</u> story, recounting the central storyline, (not a chapter by chapter summary,) including the ending.
10. Name and introduce the main characters, (in capitals at their first mention.)
11. Describe the book's location and era.
12. Mention any major scenes or crises.
13. Include character emotion and motivation.

14. Be written in story form rather than factual.
15. Be in present tense.
16. Be in third person. (he/she/his/hers.) Even when your book is written in first person.
17. Be clear and straightforward.
18. Be accurate and without typos, poor spelling or grammatical errors.
19. Be as well written as the book itself.

So you can see from that list that your synopsis is a big deal and will take several drafts. I promise you, it really will be worth the effort!

[cwb23.3] **Now write your synopsis.**

Approach this in the same way as you have for the rest of your book – *as a first draft that can be improved.*

I will reiterate here that this process can be an extremely beneficial one, really cementing the order and progression of your book, and enabling you to pick out the key characters and elements.

An example of the beginning of a synopsis is offered below, to give you an idea of tone and layout:

## 'Don't Call Me Mum!' (Published by Autonomy Press)

*Why does society always 'blame the parents' when children and adolescents display 'problem behaviour?'*

This true story shines light on SARAH'S perspective and her life

75

bringing up TOM. The story begins with a prologue, where Sarah is making desperate phone calls to Tom's Pupil Referral Unit and then to Social Care to say she can no longer cope with her fifteen-year-old son and can't have him back home.

She is reminded of her parental responsibilities and threatened with further action, rather than help, which follows the pattern she has always known.

The story then returns to 'the beginning,' with Tom's birth in 1994. Immediately Sarah is aware of his inability to sleep and his fractiousness. By the time he is six months, sleep deprivation is one of the factors that breaks up Sarah's relationship with Tom's father, PETER and she becomes a single mother…

Good luck!

# Writing your Cover Letter

You will be pleased to know that this next task is a little easier than the last one! And just as important.

Part of the submission package you will assemble, to 'sell' your story to an agent or publisher, will be your cover letter. This will be the first thing they will look at and should therefore be absolutely flawless.

If possible, address the recipient by name, using salutations. Double check for accuracy and make sure you include all your contact information. You should mention it is a memoir or autobiography, and give the title at the start of your letter.

Ideally, fit the letter onto one page and offer the 'pitch' of your book in your first paragraph. The pitch is a short statement that encapsulates the essence of your book.

For example, the pitch for my memoir is.

> *'A mother's story of being pushed to the brink by her ADHD son.'*

You should have your pitch firmly lodged in your mind anyway. If anyone asks you about your book, you need to be able to answer concisely and consistently.

The next paragraph should offer the word count and confirmation of completion. It ought to be finished before submission, unless you are entering your book into a competition, where support to edit is part of the prize.

You should have knowledge of where it sits in the marketplace and why you have made this decision. You should also be aware of which readers might like to buy it and add this information in.

Next comes your own biography as a writer. Try to offer a hint of your personality. You might talk about *why* you write, along with any successes you have in your writing history.

Finally, this letter can reassure a prospective agent or publisher of your willingness and ability to help with marketing. This could include information about your web presence and any media contacts you may have.

They are not as difficult to write as the synopsis, but still need several revisions. When you get to the point of submission, they will need adapting for each publisher or agent, depending on what they ask for within their submission guidelines.

[cwb24.1] Below is a suggested outline for structuring your cover letter. Start by making some notes alongside the bullet points so you have the content for your letter before you write the first draft.

**Opening Paragraph**

Include the following:

- The title of your story and its theme. At this stage you need to show the publisher or agent what type of book you have written so they can decide whether it will fit into their current list.
- A line or two which captures the essence of the book. This should be a concise and targeted summary.

**Paragraph Two**

Include the following:

- The book's approximate word count
- A confirmation of its completion, or when it will be finished.
- One or two comparative titles to enable agents and publishers to know whether your book is a product they can sell.
- What is its 'Unique Selling Point?' What will interest readers about it?

**Paragraph Three**

Include the following:

- Talk about you as a writer – market yourself! Try to offer a hint of your personality through your writing.
- Include a brief biography in relation to your writing career.
- Include any publishing or competition successes.

**Paragraph Four**

Include the following:

- Add information about your web presence
- Acknowledge how you will be involved in the marketing of your book.
- Include any unique media contacts you may possess.

I usually end with a comment as to why I have chosen that particular publisher, just to make it more personal.

The cover letter is your opportunity to showcase how fabulous you are, so don't hide your light under a bushel!

[cwb24.2] **Now write yours!**

# Presenting your Manuscript

It is essential that your story, along with your cover letter and synopsis is professionally presented and error free.

I would advise looking at some published books to get a sense of layout, line indents, paragraph spacing, etc.

Publishers will differ slightly in their requirements, however, if you follow the guidance below when presenting work, you will be giving it the best chance of getting through the first hurdle of passing the presentation test with an agent or publisher.

Publishers and literary agents are inundated with submissions and are possibly looking for reasons to reject your manuscript – therefore the first thing they will scrutinise will be professional presentation. Don't fall at the first hurdle! Here's a 'checklist' for you to follow to ensure you present your manuscript to the highest standard.

## Cover Sheet

First, include an overall cover sheet which includes your name and contact information, the book title, genre and word count.

## Chapter Headings

Make sure these are consistent throughout your novel, in terms of whether they are emboldened, underlined, capitalised or centred. If chapters are numbered, they should either be numbers or words (one, two) throughout.

## Font

Make sure the font is legible, (12 point is usual) and consistent throughout your novel, use Aerial or Times New Roman. Text should be double spaced throughout and left aligned. (Never fully justified.)

## Margins

Standard margin size on A4 is 2.54cm on all sides.

## Presentation

All pages should be numbered. Furthermore, they should all have a header set, (in a smaller font size than the main text,) that gives the author name and the book title in italics.

## Layout

Paragraphs do not need a gap between them. Only leave a space if there is a change of section. There is no need to use * to indicate a section break unless it occurs at the top or bottom of a page.

Never indent the first line in a new chapter or the first line after section break. The beginning of every paragraph should be indente

This includes paragraphs that consist of dialogue.

**I'll reiterate how important it is to ensure that your manuscript (or sample of it,) cover letter and synopsis are flawless.**

Where possible, you could consider getting them looked over by a professional editor or proof-reader. At the very least, get one or two trusted and reliable sets of eyes on them.

Other readers will spot things you can't, as you do become very close to your own manuscripts! I've been amazed at what comes up at this stage that I've missed myself!

Enjoy this part of your life story's journey – it means you're nearly there. You must be very excited and feeling proud of yourself!

# Performing Your Work

Now that you're nearly at the end of your life story course, you may be thinking about 'living as a writer' and immersing yourself as much as possible in the world of writing. Literature festivals offer amazing opportunities to network with other writers, attend writing workshops and listen to published writers.

But literature festivals are often infrequent annual events, so open mic (spoken word) events can offer something more regular, and can build your confidence by putting your work and your writing self out there.

This building of your confidence is vital in preparing you for virtual and in-person promotional events, such as your book launch, where you would be expected to read your work to a captive audience.

**There are several advantages of attending open mic and other spoken word events:**

- Being able to showcase your work and yourself as a writer
- Becoming part of a community and network
- Living as a writer and improving confidence
- Listening and watching the styles of other writers and becoming more familiar with trends

- Being less isolated as a writer

**Nerves can be a problem, so below are a few tips of how to overcome them**

- Knowing that your work is the best it can be.
- Becoming familiar with the use of a microphone.
- Rehearsing it at home, if possible in front of a mirror and timing yourself. (Usually you will be given 3-5 minutes – long enough to read a short scene or a short chapter.) Note any occasions of stumbling over words.
- Going 'first' can make you feel as though you are getting it out of the way, but by listening to several other writers before it is your turn, you give yourself time to focus outside yourself, and get a feel for the theme and content.
- This wait time can be used for regulating your breathing.
- Wine is good!!

**Whilst reading:**

- Ensure your position is comfortable, and the right distance in relation to the microphone.
- Remember to breathe!
- Read your work slowly and clearly, pausing where necessary to allow the words to sink in – overcome the temptation to rush.
- Imagine yourself as a 'vehicle' for your work – as though the words are emerging from behind you, and are just travelling through you, to meet your audience.
- Look up from your page every so often – look out across your audience.
- Hold a book or a folder containing your work – the 'shakes' will be

less obvious. I remember my first time of reading in public – the shakes were dreadful!

- Ensure you read a piece where the audience will be in no doubt where it ends. There's nothing worse than reading a piece and there being a silence instead of applause at the end because your audience didn't realise you'd finished! I always say 'thank you' when I've reached the end of my reading.
- Congratulate yourself afterwards – now is the time you can reward yourself with another glass of something!

Remember, it will not always be so nerve-wracking – all writers have to read for the first time somewhere!

Writers are generally a friendly and supportive bunch, and you will probably get a few of them saying positive things about your piece when you mingle afterwards.

# Getting Your Work into Print

Each writer has their own definition of success, for some, it might be their autobiographical story is enjoyed by family and friends.

For others, it might be just having their book stocked in a local bookshop, whilst some writers may aspire to the production of their memoir for the mass-market.

To achieve the latter, it is a good idea to write shorter prose such as flash fiction, short stories or poetry for submission. These are great for building up a 'CV' of writing successes, and will do wonders for your confidence as a writer, whilst additionally making you an attractive proposition for prospective publishers.

All shortlists and longlists, not just 'first prize wins,' count when building your writing CV.

There is no feeling like seeing your work in print. Soon you will be able to hold your book in your hands and I am really excited for you. Here are some ideas to bring you closer to this point:

**Subscription to a regular writing magazine**

Magazines offer information about national and international competition opportunities, as well as details of publishers seeking particular types of submission. Writing magazines also offer their own submission opportunities and regular offerings about craft and 'living as a writer.'

## Writing Competitions

Internet searches will yield a variety of writing competitions. Memoir and autobiography opportunities are few, but some short fiction success can help build your all-important writing CV.

## Literary Agents

A literary agent is paid to represent you, (usually at a fee of 15% of book sales,) and also to negotiate the best deal on your behalf. An internet search or the *Artist's and Writer's* Yearbook will list agents who are looking for memoir and autobiography submissions.

## Publishers

Again, internet searches and *The Artist's and Writer's Yearbook* will list national and international publishers that accept submissions of memoir and autobiography. You should trawl through the listings to check that they are open for submissions and that they will accept unagented submissions. (They usually take a fee of up to 20% of book sales.)

## Popular Magazines

There are many opportunities to get extracts of your life story into magazines, particularly in women's magazines. They pay quite well for short real-life anecdotes as well as fiction. It is an excellent way to build up your list of successes.

## Independent Publishing

This way you bypass the gatekeepers, (agents, competitions and publishers,) and get your work straight in front of your readers. There are associated costs, but you get to keep hold of more of the profit. (Kindle Direct Publishing offers an opportunity to enrol into Kindle Unlimited, which pays a 70% royalty.) You can produce your book as a paperback, or as an e-book, or both.

The most important point to remember is that to compete with other books out there, your book must be indistinguishable from anything that is traditionally published.

You may wish to order a box of author copies at an author discount to sell directly to your family and friends, and for any launch events and promotions you organise.

The following points should be kept in mind:

- Your writing must be polished and edited (preferably professionally.)
- Your book cover should be professionally designed.
- You will need to do research into the formatting process.
- You will need to be prepared to invest into marketing such as Amazon advertising or Facebook advertising to get your work in front of readers.

cwb25.1] **Decide on which course of action most interests you and**

**begin doing some research into the initial steps.** For example, if you know you would prefer a literary agent to act on your behalf and find your publisher, begin by researching agents who will deal with autobiography and memoir.

If you would like to begin to build your CV as a writer, list some upcoming competitions and invitations to be included in anthologies that you can enter and submit to.

# Author Platform

An author 'platform' has two elements; the *offline* one consisting of real, physical writing communities you can belong to, such as writing groups and writers' circles or literary events you can attend.

Then there's the *online* element which consists of social media, blogging and having a website.

## Social Media

There are many social media platforms around, (e.g. Pinterest, Instagram, LinkedIn,) but I would suggest for writers the two that are most worthy of being concentrated on are Facebook and Twitter.

## Facebook

Great for networking and building community. It is the platform where people over forty seem to congregate which might be useful, depending on your target readership.

Facebook can be used for creating 'events,' advertising your books and sharing publishing successes, as well as posing questions and interacting in the many writing forums which exist.

When starting out as a writer on Facebook, befriend other writers, and join Facebook groups that interest you.

## Twitter

Good for building your writing brand and showcasing authority in the area or theme you are writing in. The demographic is slightly younger than Facebook, probably age thirty to fifty.

When starting out as a writer on Twitter, again follow other writers, publishers, publications, agents, literary festivals, book bloggers, and competitions that interest you. You can follow anyone, and anyone can follow you.

Social media can be extremely time consuming and you must implement a time limit, perhaps twenty minutes of scrolling through your news feeds each day. I try to cap my usage at thirty minutes a day, but often fall down rabbit holes!

It can be effective for learning about submission opportunities, competitions and writing events. It's also a way for writers to support and promote one another.

The rule of thumb is eighty/twenty – that is eighty percent interacting with other posts, and sharing general information about writing, and twenty percent self-promotion of yourself and your work.

A prospective publisher or agent would expect you to be on at least on social media channel and able to use it for advertising your work and being able to promote events. It is even more vital if you are considering independent publishing.

## Blogging

This is an excellent way to showcase your writing ability and can be used to educate, inform, or inspire others, whilst building a following of potential readers.

You could blog on the craft of writing, or living as a writer; some writers blog on travel, food or perhaps something related to the type of memoir they write. For example, a travel writer might blog about places they visit, whilst someone writing their memoir about difficult relationships might offer a self-help way of dealing with things through their blog.

I 'double up' with my blog in that I also record it onto YouTube for those who prefer to watch and listen. This repurposing of content also increases potential readers of my books.

Using keywords throughout a blog can be a great way to bring people to your website through Search Engine Optimisation (SEO) and get them interested in something else you can offer, (like your autobiography!) I'm not going to try to explain SEO here, but there is plenty of expertise out there.

## Having a Website

A website is your shop window as a writer. It should offer information about <u>you</u>, your successes, your news, publications, blog and anything else you have to offer – for example, you might want to make yourself available to 'speak' in front of an audience, or to buddy up with another writer to swap extracts to critique.

You should put something out there of your personality. Gone are the days where we writers can hide behind a screen, readers now want to get to know us as much as possible.

Consider Wordpress to host your website. Their support is good, and the basic websites are free. You can also host your blog here. It tends to be straightforward to set up, which is what you need when you are first starting out

You can, of course, pay someone to set up the techy side of things, but I do advocate learning the processes from the ground up first and then you will know exactly what is involved when your book sales are soaring and you have plenty of revenue to call in the experts!

Decide what your initial course of action will be to get your online presence up and running. [cwb26.1]

# Living as a Writer

Now that you've reached the end of this course, you will have gained new skills, confidence, and hopefully a writing discipline.

It could be helpful to consider where you go from here. Below are a few suggestions, drawn from the last few sections of the course.

Subscriptions to a writing magazine – these will keep you informed about opportunities and events, whilst being an excellent source for continued learning.

Open mic and spoken word nights – a chance for you to gain confidence reading your writing to an audience.

Develop your on-line author platform – essential but give yourself plenty of time to develop at least one social media platform, a basic website and a blog.

Attend further courses – look out for workshops at literature festivals and for writing days.

Aim even higher and consider an OU, BA or MA in Creative Writing or other accredited course.

Attendance at literature festivals. They are widely held in March and October. Packed with workshops and inspirational speakers, they also usually hold a competition and offer networking opportunities.

Making submissions – you could make a promise to yourself that you'll submit some of your writing to a magazine, newspaper or competition on a regular basis. Perhaps each month. As mentioned before, this will build up your writing CV.

Manuscript appraisal – you could consider having your manuscript professionally critiqued. Make sure you have got it to the best place you can on your own before you submit it. A writing buddy can be brilliant for peer assessment, whereby you can improve each other's work.

Forming or joining a writing group – writing can be a lonely and solitary activity, therefore joining an established writing group can be an excellent way to stay connected to other writers. It also offers the opportunity to help one another and provide feedback to one another. If there isn't one in your area, consider starting one up of your own.

[cwb27.1] If you didn't set any goals in the previous section, do it now. If you did, set some more. Consider what you want to have achieved in the next month, three months, six months, etc. Be specific and realistic. Give yourself targets.

These could be related to your writing craft or to your professional development. Ensure they are Specific, Measurable, Attainable, Realistic and Timed. (S.M.A.R.T.)

**You have now completed 'Write your Life Story in a Year.' Well done! Your final instruction is to raise a glass in celebration of all**

**your hard work and achievement. Keep it up and happy editing!**

## Before you go...

Join my 'keep in touch' list to receive a free book, and to be kept posted of other freebies, special offers and new releases. Being in touch with other writers is one of the best things about being an author and creative writing teacher.

Visit www.mariafrankland.co.uk to join and receive a free copy of The 7 S.E.C.R.E.T.S. to Achieving your Writing Dreams.

I'd love to know what you thought of Write your Life Story in a Year, and always welcome feedback, both positive and not-so-positive! The easiest way to do this is by leaving a review, and you can leave one by revisiting the Amazon product page.

It's great to know what you want more of, or not, as the case may be! It only needs to be a line or three, but also helps other writers find the book.

## Thank you!

This book is derived from a year-long online course which includes video, access to an online support group, further writing tasks and examples, links to further reading and the option of one-to-one support.

See https://mariafrankland.co.uk/write-your-life-story/ for more information.

# By the Same Author

**How-to Books for Writers**
Write a Novel in a Year
Write a Collection of Poetry in a Year
Write a Collection of Short Stories in a Year

**Memoir**
Don't Call me Mum! A mother's story about being pushed to the brink

**Psychological Thrillers**
Left Hanging: What price would you pay to save your marriage?
The Man Behind Closed Doors: The other side of domestic bliss
The Yorkshire Dipper: What would you risk to bring the truth to the surface?
The Last Cuckoo: When ghosts live on in stepfamilies
Hit and Run: He was dead before she really knew him
The Hen Party: First there were ten. Then there were nine

**Poetry**
Poetry for the Newly Married 40 Something: How to get from Tinde to altar

# Acknowledgements

I'd like to say a huge thank you to my husband, Michael, for his support and expertise in the latter stages of this book.

Thanks also to all the writers who have taken this course over the years, either in the classroom or by distance learning. Your feedback has enabled me to tweak and refine the course, and many of you have become friends too!

Thank you to Prince Henry's Grammar School in Otley for the space and platform to offer my creative writing courses, and I also want to acknowledge Leeds Trinity University where I completed my teaching and English degree, and then my Masters in Creative Writing.

These degrees took me to a new level as a writer and enabled me to pass on my own learning through the courses I've written and now offer.

And lastly, can I thank you, the 'student' of this book, for choosing to share your writing journey with me, and for allowing me to share what I know to help you write your own life story. It is a true honour and I hope you will keep me posted of your success!

# About the Author

Maria Frankland's life began at 40 when she began making a living from her own writing and became a teacher of creative writing. The springboard into making writing her whole career was made possible by the MA in Creative Writing she undertook at Leeds Trinity University.

The rich tapestry of life with all its turbulent times has enabled her to pour experience, angst and lessons learned into the writing of her novels and poetry. She recognises that the darkest places can exist within family relationships and this is reflected in the domestic thrillers she writes. She strongly advocates the wonderful power and therapeutic properties of writing.

She is a 'born 'n' bred' Yorkshirewoman, a mother of two, and has recently found her own 'happy ever after' after marrying again. Still in her forties, she is now going to dedicate the rest of her working life to writing her own books, whilst inspiring and motivating other writers to achieve their own writing dreams.

**You can connect with me on:**

🌐 https://www.mariafrankland.co.uk

🐦 https://twitter.com/writermaria_f

📘 https://www.facebook.com/writermariafrank

🔗 https://www.autonomypress.co.uk

**Subscribe to my newsletter:**

✉ https://mailchi.mp/f69ecf568e7b/writersignup

Printed in Great Britain
by Amazon